Weather Wise

Snow

Helen Cox Cannons

raintree
a Capstone company — publishers for children

Raintree is an imprint of Capstone Global Library Limited, a company incorporated in England and Wales having its registered office at 7 Pilgrim Street, London, EC4V 6LB – Registered company number: 6695582

www.raintreepublishers.co.uk
myorders@raintreepublishers.co.uk

Text © Capstone Global Library Limited 2015
First published in hardback in 2014
Paperback edition first published in 2015
The moral rights of the proprietor have been asserted.

Edited by Siân Smith and John-Paul Wilkins
Designed by Philippa Jenkins
Picture research by Ruth Blair
Production by Victoria Fitzgerald
Originated by Capstone Global Library Ltd
Printed and bound in China Leo Paper Group

ISBN 978 1 4062 8479 9 (hardback)
18 17 16 15 14
10 9 8 7 6 5 4 3 2 1

ISBN 978 1 4062 8486 7 (paperback)
19 18 17 16 15
10 9 8 7 6 5 4 3 2 1

British Library Cataloguing in Publication Data
A full catalogue record for this book is available from the British Library.

Acknowledgements
We would like to thank the following for permission to reproduce photographs: Dreamstime: Mira Janacek, 7; Getty Images: Kristian Sekulic/E+, cover, iStockphoto: Dreef, 8, 23 (top), ParkerDeen, 9, simplytheyu, 22; Shutterstock: Gajus, 17, 23 (bottom), Kostenko Maxim, 5, KSLight, 20, Olga Miltsova, 11, oliveromg, 21, Pavel Svoboda, 19, Sunny Forest, 4, urciser, 6, vikiri, 10, Waj, 18

We would like to thank John Horel for his invaluable help in the preparation of this book.

Every effort has been made to contact copyright holders of material reproduced in this book. Any omissions will be rectified in subsequent printings if notice is given to the publisher.

Contents

What is snow?

Snow is pieces of frozen water
that fall from the sky.

These pieces of frozen water can form **snowflakes**.

Types of snow

Snowflakes fall when it is cold.
When wet snowflakes stick
together, heavy snow falls.

When it is very cold, the snowflakes
do not stick together. This is called
light snow.

Heavy snowfall with strong winds is called a **blizzard**.

Blizzards make it hard to be outside.

Is snow white?

Snow looks white, but it is not.
Snow is clear.

Snow looks white because of the light from the Sun. On a sunny day, snow is very bright to look at.

How does snow form?

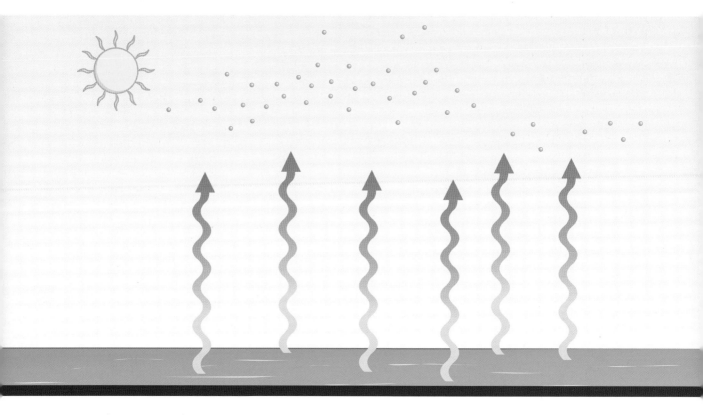

When the Sun warms water,
some of it becomes a gas
called **vapour**.

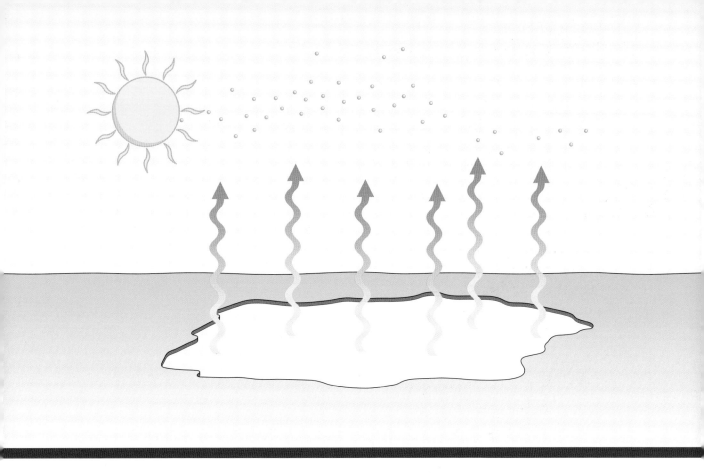

Water vapour comes from **oceans** and lakes.

The water vapour rises into the air. Then
it cools down and turns into tiny drops
of water. The tiny drops make clouds.

frozen water vapour

If it is very cold, water vapour
freezes in the clouds.

The frozen water drops join together to make snowflakes. When snowflakes get too heavy, they fall to the ground.

snowflake

Some snowflakes melt before they reach the ground. Others stay frozen because the air is so cold.

Snow around the world

Some places that have hot weather never get snow.

Some places that have cold weather get snow most of the time.

How does snow help us?

Snow brings water back to Earth.
Plants need water to grow.

Snow can be fun!

Did you know?

All snowflakes are different from each other. Snowflakes come in many different patterns.

Picture glossary

 **blizzard** period of heavy snowfall with strong winds

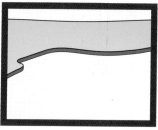 **ocean** large body of water

 **snowflake** piece of frozen water that has fallen from the sky

 **vapour** gas created by heating water

Index

Notes for parents and teachers

Before reading
Assess background knowledge. Ask: What is snow? How does snow form? How does snow help us?

After reading
Recall and reflection: Ask children how snowflakes are formed. What facts about snow surprised them?

Sentence knowledge: Ask children to look at page 6. How many sentences are on this page? How can they tell?

Word recognition: Ask children to point at the word *cold* on page 7. Can they find *cold* on page 19? Ask children to point to things in this book that are cold.

24